YOUR KNOWLEDGE HAS

Arunkumar Thangavelu

Delivering Quality Of Services For Media Streaming Networks

GRIN Verlag

Bibliografische Information der Deutschen Nationalbibliothek:

Die Deutsche Bibliothek verzeichnet diese Publikation in der Deutschen National-
bibliografie; detaillierte bibliografische Daten sind im Internet über http://dnb.d-
nb.de/ abrufbar.

Imprint:

Copyright © 2007 GRIN Verlag GmbH
Druck und Bindung: Books on Demand GmbH, Norderstedt Germany
ISBN: 978-3-640-61234-5

GRIN - Your knowledge has value

Der GRIN Verlag publiziert seit 1998 wissenschaftliche Arbeiten von Studenten, Hochschullehrern und anderen Akademikern als eBook und gedrucktes Buch. Die Verlagswebsite www.grin.com ist die ideale Plattform zur Veröffentlichung von Hausarbeiten, Abschlussarbeiten, wissenschaftlichen Aufsätzen, Dissertationen und Fachbüchern.

Visit us on the internet:

http://www.grin.com/

http://www.facebook.com/grincom

http://www.twitter.com/grin_com

Delivering Quality Of Services For Media Streaming In Group Communication Over Mobile Ad Hoc Networks (QASAN)

,Arunkumar Thangavelu, Bhuvaneswari Kandasamy, S.N. Sivanandam

ABSTRACT

The major challenge faced by designers of ad hoc network is the deployment of end-to-end quality-of-service support mechanisms for streaming media services over an adhoc group network. Group-oriented services over large ad-hoc networks has a big impact on the needs of streaming services communication in terms of mobility, quality of service (QoS) support and multicasting. In Ad hoc networks, where such features are not embedded with its architecture, it is necessary to develop QoS multicasting strategies. This paper focuses on the basic building blocks of an ad hoc group communication scheme, which achieves multicasting optimal QoS efficiency OptiQ_Policy algorithm by tracking resource availability in a node's neighborhood based on resource reservations, which announces the required QoS before each session initiation.

The primary quality of service (QoS) issues such as required bandwidth, message delay, traffic type and hop count per route improves the efficiency of streaming services over ad-hoc network. Streaming services support voice, data and video traffic by assessing and adjusting for various levels of QoS. The performance analysis is performed on functional prototype of QASAN ad hoc mobile wireless network with emphasis on service satisfaction for multiple group conference sessions.

The performance of QASAN network is well compared with QoS-aware versions of AODV [20] and TORA[17], well-known ad-hoc routing and limited QoS protocols. Using the SPRUCE[23] bandwidth traffic gathering tool, with a set of C++ modules an extensive set of performance experiments were conducted for these protocols with QASAN on a wide variety of mobility patterns and reservation strategies.

Index Terms—Quality of Services, Streaming Services, Ad Hoc Networks, group communication.

I. INTRODUCTION

QoS (Quality of Service) routing is a key network function for the transmission and distribution of digitized audio / video across next-generation high-speed networks[19]. It has two main objectives : (i) identifying routes that satisfy the QoS constraints; (ii) making efficient use of network resources. The complexity involved in the networks may require the consideration of multiple constraints to make the optimal QoS routing decision.

Most QoS protocols [6],[8],[12] proposed today purely function on best effort basis with no attempt to provide any QoS whatsoever. Routing can inform a source node of the bandwidth and QoS availability of a destination node. The notion of QoS is guarantee provided by network to satisfy a set of predetermined service performance constraints for the user in terms of the end-to-end delay statistics, available bandwidth, probability of packet loss and call admission delay.

When mobility grows high, the established routes are susceptible to link failures, diversions, or decrease of throughput. Thus, absolute throughput or delay bounds are hard to guarantee hence, some researchers have proposed the notion of Soft QoS [2] to achieve quality. Soft QoS discusses on the transient periods of time after the connection set up, where there may exist delay when QoS specification is not honoured. The level of QoS satisfaction is quantified by the fraction of total disruption time over the total connection time. This ratio should be higher than a specified threshold [1].

Algorithms that provide QoS support in AdHoc neworks should include the following features: (i) accurate measurement of bandwidth availability in the shared wireless channel; (ii) accurate measurement of effective end-to-end delay in an unsynchronized environment; (iii) distributed routing algorithm that adapts with the dynamic environment; (iv) resource

4

reservation that guarantees the available resources; (v) efficient resource release upon route adjustment; (vi) instant QoS violation detection and (vii) fast and efficient route recovery.

The task of QASAN is to identify an optimal QoS level which may be possed by a suitable path through the network or route, between the source and destination(s) that will have the necessary resources to meet the service expected by user. The task of resource request, identification, and reservation is the other indispensable ingredient of QoS. The focus of this paper is on identifying optimal QoS limit set for each session based on type of service in use. This is a complex and difficult issue because of the dynamic nature of the network topology and generally imprecise network state information. Throughout this paper the need for optimal QoS *OptiQ_Policy* for On-Demand routing service in AdHoc networks is stressed.

The remainder of this paper is organised as follows: In Section II, related works in this area are summarized. In Section III, need for optimal QoS for Ad hoc On-demand Service Group Management scheme (QASAN) is discussed. Section IV, focuses on Policy Manager and Negotiation procedures, while Section V, discusses the experimental setup procedures and and its performance analysis based on traffic rate. Finally summary and future work are presented in Section VI.

II. RELATED WORK

A. Review Stage

More and more multimedia data are being transmitted via wireless media, where such applications require diverse QoS. Due to the intrinsic scarcity of wireless bandwidth, it is challenging to provide diverse QoS while achieving high bandwidth utilization. For example, a system may allocate higher bandwidth for multimedia applications to satisfy their QoS at the expense of rejecting new calls that require less bandwidth. In order to enhance bandwidth utilization while satisfying the QoS of existing connections, numerous approaches have been proposed.

A graceful degradation mechanism is proposed by Singh [1] to increase bandwidth utilization by adaptively adjusting bandwidth allocation according to the user-specified loss profiles. For most multimedia applications (e.g., voice, video telephony or video conferencing), service can be degraded in case of congestion as long as it is still within the pre-specified tolerable range. A generic video telephony may require over 40 Kbps but low-motion video telephony requiring about 25 Kbps is acceptable [18]. Thus, a system could free some channels for new calls by lowering the QoS levels of ongoing calls. Chen et al. [14] proposed an optimal degradation strategy by maximizing a revenue function. Sherif et al. [22] proposed an adaptive resource allocation algorithm to maximize bandwidth utilization and tried to achieve fairness with a generic algorithm.

Kwon et al. [9] derived a *degradation period ratio* under the assumption that the degradation probability and mean degradation time are kept intact in all degradation states. However, these metrics are dependent on the degradation state in which a given call resides, and hence, derive a new degradation ratio. Moreover, it is shown numerically that the degradation ratio does not suffice to reflect the QoS guarantees given to individual calls.

Frequently switching among the different degradation levels may be even worse than a large degradation ratio [10]. So, we also derive a formula for switching QoS levels.

Another important issue in wireless communication is the forced-termination (or call dropping) due to non-provisioning of expected QoS probability. In case of shortage of bandwidth, hand-off calls may be dropped, thus compromising their QoS. In order to prevent ongoing calls from potential dropping/termination, Lin et al. [11] gave priority to hand-off calls over new calls, such that the forced-termination probability is improved without seriously degrading the blocking probability of new calls. Naghshineh et al. [15] proposed a distributed call admission control scheme by estimating the possible number of hand-off calls from adjacent cells.

Various reservation-based admission control schemes have also been proposed to reduce the probability of terminating ongoing or hand-off calls [8],[9]. Some optimal solutions subject to different constraints have also been proposed in [13],[24]. Slightly different from the reservation based call admission control (CAC), once the system load exceeds a predefined threshold, we restrict the traffic of newlyinitiated calls so as not to drop hand-off calls.

B. Challenges

One of the major challenges in ad hoc network systems is the deployment of end-to-end quality-ofservice support mechanisms. QASAN focuses on identifying an integrated route discovery, bandwidth provisioning, resource identification, reservation and negotiation on required QoS. QASAN is designed to operate within a TDMA network. Unlike other path finding and route discovery protocols that ignore the impact of the data link layer, QASAN incorporates dynamic session scheduling method which ensures end-to-end QoS for the type of service call.

III. QASAN ARCHITECTURE

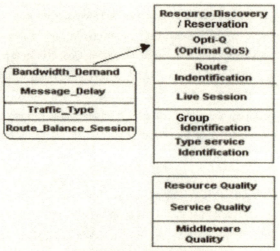

Fig-1 QASAN Stack Architecture

QASAN works on multi-cast request and reply query process. QASAN architecture is as shown in Fig-1. To provide optimal QoS, QASAN integrates (i) on-demand route discovery between the source and destination; (ii) signaling functions for resource reservation and maintenance and (iii) Identification of optimal QoS routing path. Due to the dynamic feature of Wireless AdHoc network, the connection (or session) maintenance overhead (which includes violation detection, recovery and connection tear-down of the old path) RSVP protocol [25] cannot be used. Due to the limited bandwidth usage in wireless networks, end-to-end signaling should be kept at a minimum. To reduce signaling overhead, an in-band signaling approach is proposed as in [14], with the specified group network.

The QASAN scheme follows hierarchial stack setup [Fig-1]. It has multiple phases, which focuses mainly on:

1. Group Creation (Node Discovery / Neighbour Identification / Group Discovery)
2. Route Exploration (route discovery, route repair, and route deletion)

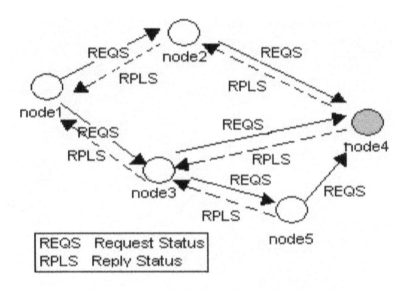

Fig-2 Node Communication

3. Optimal –QoS (OptiQ_Policy)
4. Resource Discovery and Reservation.

QASAN, adopts the following design decisions which can reduce the connection maintenance overhead:

(1) To detect and facilitate optimal QoS at the destination or intermediate nodal points among the flow's actual QoS, without the need of additional signaling, adhoc resources should be discovered;

(2) Routing adjustment overhead due to QoS violations, is reduced by employing destination-initiated recovery;

(3) Instantaneous session management procedure is used for connection creation, refresh and tear-down process using Policy Manager.

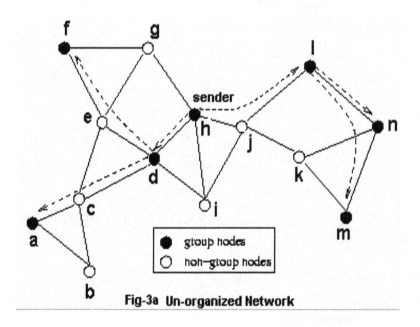

Fig-3a Un-organized Network

(4) Temporary reservation mechanism helps in reusing the old route before optimal QoS adjustment, which eliminates delay.

(5) To determine the optimal resource, route and achieve at optimal QoS, parameter policy negotiation among middleware components should be adopted.

The prime module of QASAN is Opti-Q which detects behavior of other nodes and routes traffic around the faulty nodes also well isolates them from the network. Each node observes its neighborhood and reports un-expectable behavior to the other nodes. Each node maintains a reputation table profiling the other nodes. The reputation value is updated based on the node's own observations based on service and QoS issues in use and the information provided by the other nodes. If the reputation value drops below optimal QoS threshold, the node does not provide services to faulty behaving node requests.

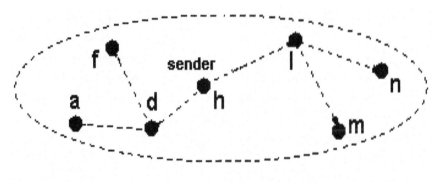

Fig-3b Associative Group

.A. QASAN Group Create / Modify

AdHoc nodes does not adpt any infrastructure or topology format. All nodes are under mobility and under constant communication with each other. Each adhoc node in the network may belong to a group or zone as per the location of node or type of service to be provided. All the nodes in a network possess the same property and methods.

Each node communicates with its neighbor node by issuing REQS (Request Status Signal), similar to Hello message protocol [12]. The receiver node 4 replies with a RPLS (Reply Status) message as in Fig2. To create a group "Node Associativity" process takes place. Fig-3 explains Node Associativity process where two adhoc networks A and B (Fig-3a), possessing multiple wireless nodes merges together to from an individual network (Fig-3b). Node Associativity is a node's association with its neighbors over time and space.

Associativity indicates connection stability. It also takes into account the battery life of nodes in the route. Beacon signals, which carry information such as the identity of the originator and its battery life, are sent out by each node and measure associativity. The more beacon signals a node receives from its neighbors over time and space, the more stable it is likely to be. If a node is moving away from its neighbors, it will receive fewer beacon signals from them. Therefore, threshold can be defined where a certain number of received beacon signals reflect instability (i.e., nodes in transition and links breaking) or stability (i.e., nodes moving but constantly connected). Hence, *associativity*, measured by the number of beacon signals from neighbors, is the new routing metric found most appropriate only for ad hoc mobile wireless networks.

Associativity helps in providing controlling multiple nodes in the network to augment optimal quality of service for type of service. Any network can be segmented or nodes can be deleted or moved into another network based on service required and its corresponding parameters.

B. Route Discovery

Supporting QoS in an ad hoc environment entails the coordination of several system activities. The first is *route discovery* and *route repair*. Since ad hoc network topologies are highly dynamic, routes between two nodes often need to be produced or discovered upon demand, at the time of connection establishment in the case of a QoS connection, since previous routes may no longer exist.

When a source node needs a route to a destination, it transmits a neighbor broadcast query for Node Identification and Status request (REQS) packet. Nodes which receive the query check to see if they are the destination, if not, the protocol appends the receiving node's information to the packet and rebroadcasts to the neighboring node Ni. The appended information includes identification, associativity with all its neighbors, route-relaying load, link-propagation delay, remaining power life, route hop count. The succeeding node erases its upstream node's associativity information with other neighbors, retaining only the portion that concerns itself and the upstream node. When nodes join a session with available QoS, this information is updated to all the neighboring most appropriate routes.

NEIGHBOR DISCOVERY
Source A:
1: send message HELLO(Ni) // request neighbor using hello
                          // protocol multicast to neighbors

Neighbor B,C,D :
1: recv message (A)
2: ackn message (A,Bid,St[B],Bw[B]) // *session time and*
                                     bandwidth of B
3: ackn message (A,Cid,St[C],Bw[C]) // *session time and*
                                     bandwidth of C
4: ackn message (A,Did,St[D],Bw[D]) // *session time and*
                                     bandwidth of D
// Bid - Identity of node B session time- time (msecs) message // received
// Bw - assigned bandwidth for node B or C or D

5: send message REQS ( )
/* 1. Any node which has the maximum no of entries in a
domain and with maximum bandwidth is considered as the
Domain Co-ordinator. */
/* 2. When two or more nodes have maximum no of neighbor
entries, then negotiation is carried between them based on
maximum bandwidth and maximum available bandwidth to
determine the Domain Co-ordinator */
Source A:
1: Update_Route (Bid, Cid, Did) // update neighbor discovery table

DOMAIN DISCOVERY
Source domain Ds:
// multicast to neighbors domains
1: send message HELLO(Di) // request neighbor using hello
protocol neighbor domains Di,Dj,Dk
1: recv message (Ds)
2: ackn message (Ds,Di,St[Di],Bw[Di]) // session time and
bandwidth of Di
3: ackn message (Ds,Dj,St[Dj],Bw[Dj]) // session time and
bandwidth of Dj
4: ackn message (Ds,Dk,St[Dk],Bw[Dk]) // session time and
bandwidth of Dk

Table-1 : Algorithm – Neighbor & Domain Discovery

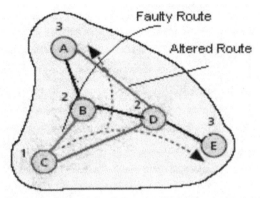

Fig-4 Faulty Route on repair / Altered Route

C. Routing Table Update

Each contacted node Ni appends its own QoS status information to the reply message RPLS. When the reply message finally reaches the destination, it contains information about all intermediate nodes Ni along that particular path. Fig-1 shows the format of a REQS message format and Fig-2 shows the format of a RPLS message.. After receiving the first RPLS message, the destination identifies the best optimal route, using *OptiQ_Policy algorithm*. OptiQ_Policy algorithm can analyze and identify optimal QoS routes based on QoS requirements as in Table-1. Route-quality parameters are used to evaluate the degree to which QoS requirements have been met. Once the protocol selects the route, the destination notifies the source and the INs of the selected route with a REPLY packet via the selected route.

The REPLY packet sends to all nodes in the route the addresses of their upstream and downstream neighbors. The downstream addresses are tagged onto the data packets for data transfer. The data packets are then relayed to the destination hop by hop.

D. Alternate Route on Repair

When links of the established route break, the protocol performs a real-time partial route repair (indicated in RED –Fig-4). Partial repair ensures that repair operations remain local, without affecting ongoing communications which is carried out by selecting an alternative route (indicated in BLUE). The operation for discovering an alternative route resembles that of route discovery described earlier, except that it is now a partial route discovery. The node detecting the route breakage initiates a localized query (LQ), rather than the source node performing media transfer.

Route repair is concerned with finding a new route during the lifetime of a connection, because the existing route has "broken", due to node mobility or transmission impairment. The second activity of route repair is *resource reservation* for providing expected QoS connections. This often involves allocation of resources at the data link or MAC level.

E. Route Deletion

After establishing an ABR route, the protocol forwards data packets along the route. However, when the source node no longer requires the route, the protocol deletes the route for two main reasons. First, whether or not data are transferred, overhead repair operations must maintain the route when movement occurs. Second, caching the route may be pointless, as node movement can invalidate the cached route. Based on the list of destinations, a node constructs a packet distribution tree using our tree construction algorithms, with the goal of minimizing the overall bandwidth cost of the tree. This overlay packet distribution tree provides us with a flexible structure to perform transport and application level packet processing and routing, yet retains low bandwidth costs similar to those of a router-assisted multicasting scheme.

IV. QASAN POLICY MANAGER (OPTIQ_POLICY)

The QASAN Policy Manager algorithm monitors, controls and identfies the effective optimal QoS by route guidance, feedback mechansim. Identifying the optimal QoS works on effective resource discovery based on expected Services. The Policy Manager negotiates on the available parameters such as bandwidth (OptiBw), hop count (OptiHc), delay (OptiDl), required rate of packet loss (OptiPl), and rqeuired session live time (OptiSess). Policy Manager provides the effective route at the time of session establishment. The QASAN Frame from each router determines the required optimal parameters on request as shown in Fig5.

OPTIMAL QoS DISCOVERY (Intra Domain Optimal QoS)

1: Send_OptiQ (A) // send optimal QoS to domain co-ordinator

2: Update OptiQ(OptiBw, OptiDl, OptiEr, ...) // OptimalQ parameters

3: OptiQ $\subset$ Negotiate_OptiQ(N[i], N[j], N[j+1]) // Negotiate with other nodes

4: OptiQ $\subseteq$ Negotiate_OptiQ(Dm[i], Dm[j], Dm[j+1]) // Negotiate with other domains 'Dm'

Table-2 OptiQ QoS Discovery

SERVICE DISCOVERY ALGORITHM

// Domain Co-ordinator maintains the information of all services in

// neighbors and neighboring domains in routing table

Domain Co-ordinator A:

1: REQS(A,N[i]) // Request for status of destination node 'i' from
   // source node A

2: RPLS(N[i], Bw[i], Dl[i], S[i]) // Reply from node 'i' with
   // Bandwidth 'Bw' in use, Delay 'Dl' for service and
   // Type of service 'S' in use.

3: UpdateRouteTable(A)

Table-3 Algorithm – Service Discovery

Policy_Manager NEGOTIATE ON OPTIMAL QoS Parameters

1: if DBw < max(Bw[Ni],Bw[Nj], ..) // required demanded bandwidth // is less than available bandwidth of node Ni

2: OptiBw = DBw // Demand bandwidth

    Else OptiBw = avlBw // Available Bandwidth

    // Negotiation on other parameters

3: OptiBw = max (Bw[Ni],Bw[Nj], ..)

4: OptiDl = $\sum$ { min(Dl[Ni], Dl[Nj],...) $\in$ S[k]) } where k $\subset$ S for all

$$t=1 \text{ to } \alpha$$

5: OptiBy = max(By[Ni], By[Ni], ...) // optimal node transmission

6: OptiPl = min (Pl[i],Pl[j], ...) // Packet Loss obtained from History

7: OptiSess = max (St[i],St[j], ...) // maximum session time in a node

$$\text{// to select the optimal QoS}$$

8: OptiQ = $\sum$ (OptiBw and OptiDl) $\parallel$ (OptiBy $\parallel$ OptiSess) $\cup$

$$(\text{OptiPl})$$

Table 4- Algorithm – Policy Manager – Negotiate on QoS

Policy_Manager NEGOTIATE_ON_OptiQ (send_slots (Ni) ,

recv_slots (Nj))

// Negotiate on AdHoc Network and AdHoc nodes

1: free_recv_slots(node A) =^(send_slots(node A) |

$$\text{recv\_slots(nodeA))}$$

2: free_send_slots(node A) = free_recv_slots(node A) ^

$$\text{recv\_slots(node A neighbors)}$$

3: send_slots(node X) = HELLO(send_slots(node X))

4: recv_slots(node X) = HELLO(recv_slots(node X))

5: free_slots(node X) = HELLO(free_slots(node X))

6: recv_slots(node A) = 0;   7: recv_slots(node A neighbors) = 0

8: for (each neighbor N of node A)

{

   recv_slots(node A) = recv_slots(node A) | send_slots(node N)

   recv_slots(node A neighbors) = recv_slots(node A neighbors) |

   recv_slots(node N)

}

9: send_link_bandwidth (A sends to X) = free_send_slots(node A) &

                                 free_recv_slots(node X)

10: recv_link_bandwidth (A recv from X) = free_recv_slots(nodeA)

                             & free_send_slots(node X)

11: receive link bandwidth NA (A receives from N)

12: index of N's neighbor M, where M is next hop in routing table

13: receive link bandwidth MN (N receives from M)

14: index of M's neighbor P, where P is next hop in routing table

entry for the destination X, at node M path bandwidths NA, MN and PM.

Table-5 Policy_Manager -OptiQ QoS

Route Frame

Ni in use	Domain Di in use	Next Dj Domain	Bandwidth in use	Hop count

QoS Frame

Req Delay	Bandwidth on Demand	ToS	Bandwidth Available	Message Delay

Fig-5 QASAN Route & QoS Frame

V. QoS Simulation Evaluation Metrics

Metrics play the vital role in evaluation of quality of service for ad hoc routing protocols. Based on a detailed study [4], [8], various QoS metrics have been identified based on bandwidth measurement, we propose a new evaluation metric which expresses the bandwidth efficiency.

$$BWER^1 = TransmittedPackets / ReceivedPackets$$

Transmitted packets are different from sent packets in the way that sent packets can be dropped for different reasons such as unreachable destination whereas transmitted packets can be dropped only because of collisions or bandwidth buffer overflow. Number of sends includes the packets that are sent to a route which does not anymore support the level of QoS required to a destination. This type of packets will eventually be dropped due to link congestion. BWER shows the total amount of bandwidth that source nodes use to deliver the goodput (excluding the packets sent to invalid routes).

Packet delay is another evaluation metric that is used for measurements. This metric shows the average packet latency to be successfully delivered to the destination node. The value of this metric can evaluate the performance of different protocols for real-time applications. To measure the cost of QoS extension, we proposed a metric to evaluate the overhead of QoS AODV and to compare it with overhead in AODV routing protocol. Overhead is usually measured as the number of control packets transmitted to establish and maintain the paths in a network. The unseen side of overhead in most of the previous publications is the amount of resources wasted due to imprecise routing information, such as the sub-optimal routing overhead [18] and dropped packets. In this work we focus on the

---

[1] BWER = Bandwidth Efficiency Ratio

second mean of overhead in addition to control routing overhead. We define Normalized Overhead Load (NOL) as following:

$$NOL = TotalOverhead(Bytes) / DeliveredPackets(Bytes)$$

where the total amount of overhead in AODV protocol includes control routing packets and the amount of wireless bandwidth wasted to transmit the packets that are dropped in other links. This value in QoS-AODV includes the amount of control routing packets as well as QoS routing control packets such as ICMP-QoS lost.

A. Capacity estimation

In multi-hop wireless networks, flows that traverse the same geographical vicinity contend for the same wireless channel capacity. Determining the capacity of an arbitrary ad hoc network is difficult because neighboring links using the same channel interfere, and the interference relationships between all of the links in a network can be quite complex. QASAN work has addressed this question using HELLO signaling protocol, which identifies the given flow vector is feasible on a particular ad hoc network, where "feasible" means that a global scheduler with access to all the information in the network could find a link scheduling policy that would achieve the desired rates. QASAN uses the route frame as shown in Fig-5 The results have been proved using, real measurements, based on information given by wireless card driver.

B. Delay estimation

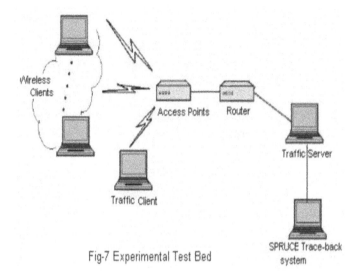

Fig-7 Experimental Test Bed

With the QASAN protocol, QoS information required for route calculation is immediately available when needed. So, before sending data traffic we must inform each node about the delay information between any node and its MPRs. The only way to calculate the delay is to use the control messages. Each node periodically broadcasts locally its HELLO messages. These control messages are transmitted in broadcast mode without acknowledgements in response. The received HELLO messages are used by each node to estimate the Expected Total Time Transmission (ETTT). The Expected Total Time Transmission is a function of Maximum queuing time, loss rate and bandwidth of the link.

C. Admission control and resource reservation

Once a path is chosen for one QoS flow, the source node cannot guarantee end-to-end QoS requirements, since paths are calculated using partial topology, and because of congestion and mobility, the validity of the path must be checked to admit a new flow at the source node. This is usually referred to as Resource Admission Control (RAC)[3][9]. A RAC can be carried out at the source or distributed at each hop in the path.

The process of RAC at each hop is more suitable for proactive protocols. Each intermediate node on the selected path checks local QoS constraints using local (vs. global) total (vs. partial) topology information (using information from HELLO messages). A node can proceed to (soft and later hard) resource reservation on the links during the RAC process. This ensures that no two flows initiated simultaneously will contend for the same resource. The bandwidth capacity, delay, rate of packet loss, call / resource admission control information gathered are addressed to neighboring adhoc nodes / domains using QASAN router frame [Fig-5].

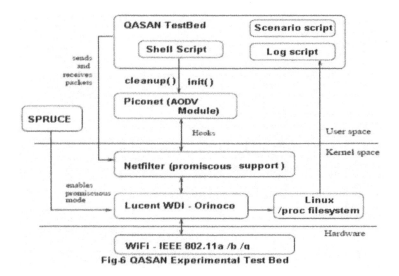

Fig-6 QASAN Experimental Test Bed

The QASAN frame is broadcasted to all neighboring domains. The updated parameters from Policy Manager module on negotiation determine the optimal QoS. Fig-6 shows both the Route Frame which gathers the router parameters in use and QoS Frame shows the quality parameters which determine the effective QoS.

VI. EXPERIMENTAL TEST BED PREPARATION

The results have been conducted with Real measurements, based on information given by wireless card driver. Other metrics, such as jitter, data loss probability, security, power consumption and others are gathered.

The routing experiments ran on top of a set of 40 Gateway Solo 9300 laptops, each with a 10GB disk, 128MB of main memory, and a 500MHz Intel Pentium III CPU with 256KB of cache. We used one laptop to control each experiment, leaving 39 laptops to actually run the ad hoc routing algorithms. Each laptop ran Linux kernel version 2.2.19 with PCMCIA card manager version 3.2.4 and had a Lucent (Orinoco) Wavelan Turbo Gold 802.11b wireless card. The cards can auto adjust transfer bit rate depending on the observed signal-to-noise ratio and auto-adjust the channel to arrive at a consistent channel for all the nodes in the ad hoc network. An ad hoc mode in which the transmission rate was fixed at 2 Mb/s, and in which the channel could be chosen manually.

A. Hardware Setup Used

The hardware setup of QASAN model is as shown in Table-6.

The tool used for simulation Spruce [23] requires careful scheduling of probe traffic. More precisely, the input gap between a pair of probes must be accurate and sometimes, as small as a few hundred microseconds. Because processes cannot sleep for intervals shorter than one kernel tick (10ms or 1ms are common values), each tool uses a delay loop that holds the processor until either preempted or done sending a train of packets. Because this delay loop effectively blocks all other programs from sending traffic for the duration of an entire modules, the tools cannot properly measure cross traffic sent from the machine on which it runs.

1) Network size	Measured as the number of nodes
2) Network connectivity	The average degree of a node (i.e. the average number of neighbors of a node)
3) Topological rate of change	The speed with which a network's topology is changing.
4) Link capacity	Effective link speed measured in bits / second, after accounting for losses due to multiple access, coding, framing, etc.
5) Fraction of unidirectional links	Effectiveness of protocol performance as a function of the presence of unidirectional links
6) Traffic patterns	Protocol effectiveness in adapting to non-uniform or bursty traffic patterns
7) Mobility	When and under what circumstances, is temporal and spatial topological correlation relevant to the performance of a routing protocol
8) Fraction and frequency	QAWN protocol performance in the presence of sleeping nodes sleeping and awakening nodes.

Table 7- QASAN Test Bed parameters

Any application that uses one of these measurement tools must therefore use some other mechanism to account for the effect of traffic sent from the same machine on available bandwidth estimates. Applications could either account for their own traffic explicitly, or operating systems could provide scheduling methods to send packets at precise intervals without holding the process.

Spruce, a tool for estimating available bandwidth and compared its performance with two existing tools, IGI[16] and Pathload[7]. Spruce is simple, and generates a relatively low amount of probe traffic. Experiments over a large number of Internet paths indicate that Spruce estimates available bandwidth more accurately than Pathload [26].

The outdoor routing experiment took place on a rectangular athletic field measuring approximately 225 (north-south) by 365 (eastwest) meters. The athletic field was selected, as it was physically distant from campus and the campus wireless network, reducing potential interference. IEEE 802.11b enabled WiFi laptops were configured to use wireless channel 9 for maximum separation from the standard channels of 1, 6 and 11, further reducing potential interference.

Totally 40 laptops were used, where 39 as application laptops, and one as a control laptop (server) where QASAN algorithm is implemented. The traffic generator on each laptop generated packet streams with a mean packet size of 1200 bytes (including UDP, IP and Ethernet headers), a mean of approximately 5.5 packets per stream, a mean delay between streams of 15 seconds, and a mean delay between packets of approximately 3 seconds. These parameters produced approximately 423 bytes of data traffic (including UDP, IP and Ethernet headers) per laptop per second, a relatively modest traffic volume, but corresponding to the traffic volume observed during trial runs of one of prototype media streaming applications [8]. All four algorithms are implemented in C++ and share a core set of classes. These classes include the event loop, as well as unicast and multicast, routing, and logging support.

B. Performance & Evaluation

From the case study above, several conclusions can be drawn on the performance of the above mentioned routing algorithms. First, QASAN outperforms AODV significantly in terms of routing overhead in low mobility (small p) and small-scale network (small N) situation. However, its performance deteriorates rapidly when the situation gets stressful, i.e. p and N increase.

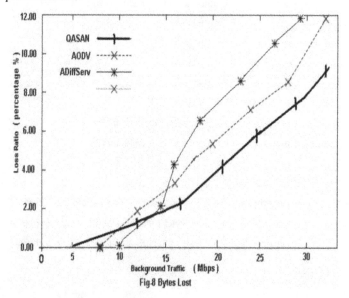

Fig-8 Bytes Lost

This is due to the aggressive usage of source routing cache. During a route discovery process, the source can learn several routes to its destination. This enables the source node to switch to cached routes in case of the currently using route break, which significantly reduced the possibility to restart a route discovery process. However, in stressful situations, it is more likely that all the cached routes are already invalid, thus introduces unnecessary delay and extra network traffic as shown in Fig-8.

Second, QASAN during multicast sustains better in more stressful condition than AODV or TORA. For once route discovery process destination node will only return one RREP packet. This enables the source node to quickly restart route discovery process to resume the transmission whenever current route fails. AODV fails in this case This is a beneficial feature in high mobility situations, where movement of nodes can quickly invalidate current route and cached route entries.

Third, in less stressful situation, multicast packets (RREQ) detoriate the routing load of AODV, whereas in QASAN multicast packets manages traffic load with Policy Manager. The reason is that in AODV destination node only replies once for one route discovery process. In most cases, failure of current route means the source node has to start another new route discovery process, which floods RREQ broadcast / multicast over the Ad Hoc network. In case of QASAN failure of a route alters the route only at the point of failure. Fourth, either protocol (QASAN or AODV) does not scale very well to network size. This can be clearly seen from Figure 9, where numbers of broadcast packets grow to several orders magnitude larger than that of unicast packets, which indicates that the network is already saturated by broadcast stream.

VII. SUMMARY

Distance Vector Routing protocols supports ad hoc mobile routing. A comparative study [3] of many routing protocols proposed to the Internet Engineering Task Force (IETF) reports that Optimal Demand on Quality Services based routing (QASAN) for group communication is superior because it is a source-initiated, on-demand for providing optimal quality scheme. The experiments show that by applying the relative QASAN scheme, both routing methods can significantly improve the probability of being able to find an end-to-end QoS path. Thus QASAN scheme demonstrates a considerable improvement over AODV protocol and its contemporary TORA, ADiffServ schemes. QASAN scheme can be implemented over wireless routers. Future works on QASAN can be focused on minimizing the percentage of packet loss and minimizing the end-to-end delay for adhoc streaming networks.

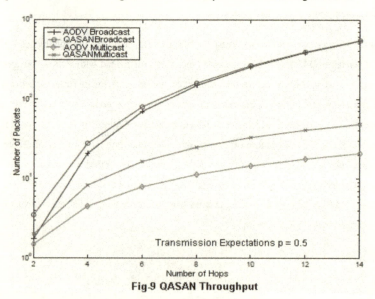

Fig 9 QASAN Throughput

REFERENCES

[1] Agarwal.S, Ahija A, J. P. Singh, and R. Shorey, Route-lifetime assessment based routing (RABR) protocol for mobile ad-hoc networks Proc. IEEE International Conference on Communications 2000 (ICC'00), Volume 3, pg 1697-1701, 2000

[2] Andrea Zanella et al, On Providing Soft-QoS in Wireless Ad-Hoc Networks, Proceedings of WPMC'03, Kanagawa, Japan, October 19-22, 2003.

[3]. Blake S, Black D, W. Weiss, An architecture for differentiated services RFC 2475, IEFT, 1998.

[4]Campbell A.T, G.S. Ahn, A. Veras, and L.H. Sun. Supporting service differentiation for real-time and best-effort traffic in stateless wireless ad hoc networks (SWAN), IEEETransactions on Mobile Computing,1(3),pg 192-207, September 2002.

[5]Crawley.E, Rajagopalan et al, RFC 2386, A Framework for QoS-Based Routing in the Internet, IETF, August 1998.

[6]Jawhar I, J. Wu, Quality of Sevice Routing in Mobile Ad Hoc Networks in Resource Management in Wireless Networking, M.Cardei Kluwer Publications, 2003.

[7]Jain Mand C. Dovrolis, Pathload: a measurement tool for end-to-end available bandwidth, in Proc of PAM, pp. 14-25, March 2002.

[8]Kia Makki, et al, Mobile and Wireless Internet: Protocols, Algorithms and Systems, Kluwer Academic Publishers, 2003, ISBN 0-7923-7208-5.

[9]Kwon T,C. Bisdikian, , Y. Choi and M. Naghshineh, Call admission control for adaptive multimedia in wireless/mobile networks, Proceedings of the First ACM International Workshop on Wireless and Mobile Multimedia, Dallas, 1998.

[10] Lin. C.R, Liu J.S, QoS routing in ad hoc wireless networks, IEEE Journal on Selected Areasin Communications, Vol 17, No. 8, pg 1426-1438, August 1999

[11] Lin C.R and J.Liu, QoS Routing in Ad Hoc Wireless networks, IEEE J. Sel. Areas Commun., vol. 17 (8), p. 1426, August 1999.

[12] Luo H, Lu S, V. Bharghavan, A New Model for Packet Scheduling in Multihop Wireless Networks, IEEE MobiCom 2000, Boston, MA, August 2000

[13] Mohapatra P, J. Li, C. Gui, QoS in Mobile Ad hoc Networks, Special Issue on QoS in Next-Generation Wireless Multimedia Communications Systems in IEEE Wireless Communications Magazine, June 2003

[14] Nahrstedt K and Chen .S, Distributed quality-of-service in ad-hoc networks, IEEE Journal on Selected Areas in Communication, 17(8), August 1999.

[15] Naghshineh. M, Marc Willebeek-LeMair, End-to-End QoS Provisioning in Multimedia Wireless/Mobile Networks Using an Adaptive Framework, IEEE Communications Magazine, November 1997.

[16] Ningning Hu, Peter Steenkiste, Evaluation and Characterization of Available Bandwidth Probing Techniques -IGP, IEEE JSAC Special Issue in Internet & WWW Measurement, Mapping, and Modeling, Vol. 21(6), Aug. 2003

[17] Park. V, S Corson, TORA QoS-Routing protocol, Temporally-Ordered Routing Protocol (TORA), IETF Internet Draft, draft-ietf-manet-tora-epc-00.txt, November 1997.

[18] Perkins C.E, Ed, Ad Hoc Networking, Addison-Wesley,2001

[19] Reed D, A Discussion on Computer Network Conferencing RFC-1324, Network working group, IETF, May 1992

[20] Royer E.M and C.E. Perkins, Quality of Service for Ad Hoc On Demand Distance Vector (AODV) Routing, IETF Internet Draft, draft-ietf-manet-aodvqos-00.txt, July 2000.

[21] Shah S, K. Chen, and K. Nahrstedt, Dynamic Bandwidth Management in Single-hop Ad Hoc Wireless Networks, Proc. of 1st IEEE Intl. Conf. on Pervasive Computing and Commn.(PerCom) 2003, Fort Worth, TX, March 2003.

[22] Sherif. M, I. Habib, M. Naghshineh, P. Kermani, Adaptive Allocation of Resources and Call Admission Control for Wireless ATM Using Genetic Algorithms, IEEE JSAC - Journal of Selected Areas in Communications, 2000

[23] Strauss J , D. Katabi, and F. Kaashoek, A measurement study of available bandwidth estimation tools, in Proc. of 2003 ACM SIGCOMM Conf. on Internet Measurement, pp. 39-44, Oct. 2003

[24]Taekyoung Kwon et al, QoS provisioning in wireless/mobile multimedia networks using an adaptive framework, Wireless Networks, Volume 9,Issue 1, pg 51-59,January 2003.

[25]Zhang L, S. Deering, D. Estrin, RSVP: A new resource reservation protocol,IEEE network, 1993.

[26]http://www.cc.gatech.edu/fac/Constantinos.Dovrolis/pathload.html.

Dr Arunkumar Thangavelu (arunkumar.thangavelu@gmail.com) is currently working as an Associate professor at the Vellore Institute of Technology - University, India. He has over 12 years of academic and R&D experience in industries. He has managed and initiated multiple national level projects including QoS for WiFi forum. He is an active consultant in R&D planning, proposal evaluation as well project reviewing a number of PG projects and PhD works.

His area of research interest focuses on mobile computing, adhoc high-performance networking, ubiquitous computing, aspect based network management which includes mobile 3G networks, ambient technologies and vehicular based applications. He has published multiple papers in international conferences and journals. He has served as chair and committee member in organizing numerous national level conferences.

Dr Bhuvaneswari Kandasamy is The Director, Department of Computer Applications, Vivekanandha Institute of Technology for Women, Tiruchengode, Tamilnadu, India. She possess more than 13 years of academic experience and has immense interest in Mathematical and Simulation Modelling and Computing, Digital Image Processing, Digital Topology and Traffic Engineering Issues in Networking. She has published good number of papers in various International Journals.